THE COMPLETE GUIDE TO QUORA

INCLUDING TIPS, USES, AND QUORA BEST PRACTICES FOR BUSINESS AND SOCIAL MEDIA MARKETING

TOM CORSON-KNOWLES

Published by TCK Publishing

www.TCKPublishing.com

**Get the free newsletter for
more marketing tips at:**

BlogBusinessSchool.com

EARNINGS DISCLAIMER

When addressing financial matters in any of books, sites, videos, newsletters or other content, we've taken every effort to ensure we accurately represent our products and services and their ability to improve your life or grow your business. However, there is no guarantee that you will get any results or earn any money using any of our ideas, tools, strategies or recommendations, and we do not purport any "get rich schemes" in any of our content. Nothing in this book is a promise or guarantee of earnings. Your level of success in attaining similar results is dependent upon a number of factors including your skill, knowledge, ability, dedication, business savvy, network, and financial situation, to name a few. Because these factors differ according to individuals, we cannot and do not guarantee your success, income level, or ability to earn revenue. You alone are responsible for your actions and results in life and business. Any forward-looking statements outlined in this book or on our Sites are simply our opinion and thus are not guarantees or promises for actual performance. It should be clear to you that by law we make no guarantees that you will achieve any results from our ideas or models presented in this book or on our Sites, and we offer no professional legal, medical, psychological or financial advice.

CONTENTS

ॐ

WHY YOU SHOULD
READ THIS BOOK

ଓଃ୫ଠ

Don't be surprised if you haven't heard of Quora before. It is relatively new to the internet scene, without the huge user base of social media giants like Facebook or Google+, but it is growing fast.

Quora provides a very different approach to social media. The focus is on helping people find answers to the questions that are important to them. Quora is much more focused on education and information than any other social network.

It was started by two former employees of Facebook, one of whom left Facebook specifically to start a website built on user-generated questions and answers.

Quora can best be explained as a cross between *Yahoo! Answers* and social media. It is a place people go to find the answers to their questions and connect with other people who have similar interests. It's also a great place for anyone who loves to share information and answers with others.

Everyone is an expert in at least one subject. Quora allows you to share your expertise with the world and be richly rewarded by the expertise of others. One person's unfathomable question may just be your life's passion, and vice versa.

Quora allows users to get their questions answered - any question at all from the meaning of life, to everyday phenomenon, to advanced questions about CSS and HTML. Quora also gives people like you and me the opportunity to share our expertise with people who are really interested and want to learn more.

This is why Quora is one of the most powerful ways for a business to connect with potential customers, because they're actively seeking out information in the area of **your** expertise. If you give them the answers they want, they'll want to do business with you. Using Quora makes it easy for these information-seekers to share your words of wisdom with the world, and therefore grow your brand and online exposure for you, free of charge.

I predict that Quora will become the #1 site in the world to go to for advice in the next few years. Yes, that's right, I think it's going to be **even more**

important than Google when it comes to getting the *right* information you need on a specific subject.

You see, Google's search rankings are based on algorithms. But Quora's Q&A system is all user-generated. That means you can't buy your way to the top of the Answer threads. The only way to succeed on Quora is to have your audience actually vote your answers as the most helpful. Although this system isn't perfect, it's a lot better than Google's search results when it comes to finding great answers to your questions.

You might be thinking by now that Quora is a lot like Yahoo! Answers, and it is. Except it's a lot better. Here's why...

Yahoo! Answers has a lot of spam, an absolutely atrocious user interface, and no way to find similar or related questions. Quora, on the other hand, has a beautifully designed website and interface, is easy to use, has incredibly helpful topics and categories, and has the ability to merge similar questions, among many other key benefits and improvements when compared to other Q&A websites. The ability to merge questions means you won't be overwhelmed with 26 variations to the same question, as you would on *Yahoo! Answers* or other similar Q&A sites.

And, on top of all that, Quora has a social network, blogging platform, points you can earn to promote your questions and answers, and many more advanced features as well.

Quora is crowdsourcing knowledge, and it's doing it in an ingenious, powerful and incredibly effective way. Yes, Wikipedia contains a huge pool of crowdsourced knowledge. But it has serious problems and drawbacks. Many companies simply pay people to change listings on Wikipedia, and because of the complex editorial nature of the site, there's almost no way to detect or prevent malicious, unethical or simple false edits on Wikipedia. The system fails because it is not transparent and the financial incentives are completely out of whack.

Quora, on the other hand, is completely transparent. You can see who wrote what answer. You can see who voted up the answers. You can even see what edits a user has made to their questions and answers. This transparency doesn't just improve the quality of the site. It improves the value of the site for every user, and especially for savvy entrepreneurs and businesses.

Quora's massive user base, combined with their focus on *high quality* answers makes it a powerful tool for people to promote themselves and their business through providing educational content and helping others. On Quora you can find a community that very much wants to learn what you know, and is eager to hear what you have to say. The process of converting these avid learners into equally avid customers and clients can be a valuable addition to your marketing plan.

Best of all, it's free to use! Unlike Facebook, you don't need to pay for people to see your content. They will see it if it's good. If people like your content, you can promote it to others for free using Quora's credit system in which promotional opportunities are earned by providing value to the network. It's a win-win system that rewards people for helping others.

There's no way to buy your way to the top on Quora. That means if you're just a solo entrepreneur or a tiny little business, you have just as much of a chance to succeed on Quora as any Fortune 500 Company. After reading this book, your chances will be a lot better!

This guide is intended as an introduction to Quora for people who use social media to promote themselves or their business. Like all social media sites, Quora provides unique opportunities and challenges to business promotion. Familiarity with the site can help with the process of establishing your presence and building a network of contacts within the Quora community.

EXPERTISE IS EVERYTHING

Customers want to buy from experts they know, like and trust. Quora allows you to be known, liked, and trusted in your areas of expertise and can lead to a lot of new customers for your business if you do it right!

Remember, social media is NOT about selling. It's about connecting, entertaining, and educating. Quora, in particular, has a huge focus on education and sharing valuable information. Entertainment is a big plus as well. When you educate your potential clients on Quora, they will come to know you as an expert in your field and will naturally buy from you when and if they need your services.

Why? Because when you solve someone's problem in a few minutes that they've probably had for weeks, months, or years, they appreciate it. There's no better way to earn trust than to provide useful information and education to someone for free.

One of the main benefits of Quora over other social media-type sites is the ability to easily demonstrate your expertise, just a few minutes at a time. By answering questions related to your field you are able to show people who might be interested in your services the value of your knowledge and eventually connect with them directly. Unlike other social media sites, people come to Quora looking for information, not necessarily social interaction (although there's plenty of that to go around, but it's nothing like Facebook or Twitter in that regard). This focus on information and not interaction can make it challenging to create connections with people, but if you are in a knowledge-driven business, the opportunity to show your knowledge directly can more than overcome this challenge.

Quora can definitely help you become known as the go-to expert in your field. **People want to do business**

with experts. We're tired of getting ripped off by mechanics, dentists, landscaping companies, and a variety of other service and product-based businesses. Consumers want expert information, they want it now, and they want it free. On Quora, you can provide that information to your target audience.

You may be thinking, *"Why should I give away all my hard-earned knowledge for free?"* Well, think about it this way...

First of all, if you don't give it away for free online, someone else will, and *they* will become known as the expert in your field, NOT you. Second, most customers won't do the work themselves. They'll either find out it's too complicated, too time-consuming, or just not worth it. So they'll want to hire an expert to do it for them.

YOU can become that expert.

UNDERSTANDING HOW QUORA WORKS

Quora is based entirely on asking and answering questions. People who are looking for information create questions that other Quora users answer. The questions are all divided into a series of topics and subtopics to make finding the subjects you are interested in much easier. You can keep track of interesting topics by following them, so topic-related activity shows up in your account feed, and you can also follow people whose answers or questions you find interesting. Like many news and information sites, Quora has "related item" links on every page. It actively promotes unanswered questions to users, in hopes that someone will be able to provide an answer.

New users may find Quora somewhat confusing. That's normal. If you remember Facebook or Twitter when they were new, then you remember the feeling of wondering what to do and how to do it.

No need to worry about that. We're going to cover all the basics you'll need to set up your account, get involved on the site, help out your target audience and become the well-known expert in your field.

Chapter 1
Your Quora Crash Course

☙☙

The goal of this guide is to give you all the tools you need to get started using Quora to promote your work. Here is a brief look at what you can find in the pages ahead:

Set Up

Setting up a Quora account is simple and straight forward. And while the site itself can be confusing, the set up process is designed to get you right into the thick of things. By the time you are done, you will have several topics and possibly some people already filling your feed with their activity.

One very good thing about Quora is that it is designed to encourage participation, so even if you aren't sure where to get started, the set up process will help you find a few places you can jump in with both feet.

ASKING AND ANSWERING QUESTIONS

Once you are done with set up, you'll want to get involved with the main business of Quora: asking and answering questions. This is the first step in connecting with other Quora users, and establishing your expertise.

COMBINING QUORA WITH OTHER SOCIAL MEDIA

Don't get involved in Quora expecting immediate results. Quora is primarily a networking opportunity, and, as with most networking opportunities, you won't see quick results. Long term participation, however, can lead to new connections and a growing customer base. By combining other social media with Quora, you can get a great deal of advantage out of your Quora activity in building your other networks.

INTERACTING WITH OTHER QUORA USERS

Of course, using Quora isn't just about it's benefits over other social media sites. There are plenty of ways to work within Quora to build connections and interact with people. We'll be taking a look at both proactive and reactive ways to interact on Quora and how each is important to building your contacts within the community.

QUORA BOUNTY OFFICE AND OTHER USER-GENERATED PROGRAMS

Part of those interactions includes familiarizing yourself with the Quora credit system, and how you can use credits to promote your answers and the answers or questions. Once you are familiar with the basics of Quora, you can also explore things like the Quora Bounty Office, which uses rewards of Quora credits to solicit well supported and valuable answers to important questions and topics.

The Quora Bounty Office is one of the newest of Quora's specialty boards, all of which are worth exploring and experimenting with. If you are feeling adventurous, you can even build your own.

LEVERAGING QUORA TO PROMOTE YOUR WORK

After we're finished reviewing Quora itself, you'll find your one-stop guide to using Quora to promote yourself and your business. This section will tie together everything else we've discussed into one easy-to-follow plan for converting Quora users, through a series of steps, into your new customers and clients.

This is what you've been waiting for—but don't skip ahead! If you want to get the most out of Quora it is important to take the time to learn about the site and it's features, before jumping in with both feet!

LIMITATIONS OF QUORA

We'll also take a look at some of the limitations of Quora. No site is perfect, and Quora has a few issues that can be downright aggravating.

IS QUORA RIGHT FOR YOU?

Finally, we'll examine ways to determine if Quora is the right tool for promoting yourself and your work. If you are unsure about whether or not Quora is a good choice for promoting your work, reading though this section can help you come to a decision.

WRAPPING UP

This guide will wrap up with a brief summary, and a quick look at some of the other ways you can use Quora. While Quora can be a powerful tool for promoting your business, there are a lot of other things you can use it for as well. Don't hesitate to explore all the advantages Quora can offer.

I hope you enjoy learning about Quora, and benefit from learning how to make it a valued part of your promotional work.

Now that you know what to expect, let's get started. First up we're taking a step-by-step look at the process of setting up your Quora account.

CHAPTER 2
SETTING UP YOUR ACCOUNT

 C8>O

Once you've decided that opening an account on Quora is the right thing for you, it's time to get set up. To actually start your Quora account all you need is your name, an email and a password. If you have them, you can also create an account using your Facebook, Google or Twitter accounts. Using one of those accounts to create your Quora will automatically tie Quora to your other social media.

CREATING YOUR ACCOUNT

When you create your account, you will be asked to confirm your email or other social media account. When you do this, Quora will access your friends, contacts or followers on that account. If any of those people are on Quora, you will be asked if you want to follow their Quora activity. Following people on Quora puts their Quora activity on your feed, just like on Facebook of Twitter. You will see the questions they ask, the answers they give and any answers from other people that they vote on.

After you have picked the people already on Quora that you want to follow, you will be asked to invite the rest of your contact list to join Quora. As usual, be careful whom you invite—no one likes getting a spammy email. Only invite the people who you know would be interested in Quora, and try to personalize the message to them.

The next step is picking five general topic areas in which you want to be involved on Quora. You can unfollow these topics later if you want, but Quora is designed to make people participate, so you have to pick at least five topics. At this point, the options are all very broad: Books, Finance, Dating and Relationships, Marketing, and Science are a few examples. You have thirty options to choose from. Pick things that interest you and relate to your business, and move on. You'll be finding the topics you really need to get involved in a bit later.

The second step of topics is picking subtopics under the five topics you selected. Each main topic will have four to five subtopics, and you need to choose a total of five subtopics. Try to choose subtopics that are related to the promotion and networking you want to do. If there isn't anything directly related, pick topics that are somewhat related, or where you might find information helpful to you.

Click the continue button after selecting your five subtopics, and you will be taken to the Quora homepage.

Action Steps

Go to **Quora.com** right now and register your account if you haven't done so already.

Your Quora Homepage

Before we continue with account set up, let's take a look over your home page.

The main section of your home page is your feed. Right now this will be filled with recent activity in the topics your selected and by the people you are following. There are two tabs at the top of your feed: Top Stories and Recent Activity. Top Stories will show you the most popular activity in your feed, and Recent Activity will show you the latest events.

Each event on your feed has:

- A headline (Answer promoted in Books or Your Contact voted up an answer in Business, for example)
- A link to the question the event is related to
- The first few lines of the question

- Answer or comment
- A link: (more). Clicking (more) will open up the full question, answer or comment on your home page.

You can Upvote or Share interesting events directly from your home page as well.

On the right side of your home page is a column including links to other areas of your Quora (Unanswered Questions in categories you are following, your inbox and a few other points of interest we'll be looking at later), Trending Topics, a link to complete your profile, and links for connecting your other social media accounts with Quora.

YOUR QUORA PROFILE

Go ahead and click on your name, under Complete Your Profile. Quora is lighter on profile details than many websites. Most of your profile will be filled with your personal feed, so people who visit your profile can easily view the questions and answers you have written. But you'll want to have a few things ready when you go to fill out the rest of your profile:

A catchy tagline that relates to your field of expertise

A recognizable avatar image; If you have other social media accounts, use the same avatar on all of them

A short "About Me" description

The tagline goes in the "Brief Bio" section of the profile, and will show up next to your name every time you post a question, answer or blog on Quora.

The avatar image will be your only picture on Quora, so make sure it is something that ties in with your main website and other social media.

The About Me description goes at the bottom when you fill in your profile, but is the first thing people see when they visit your profile page. Here is where you include links to your main website and information on the kind of work you do. Quora does not have any place to include contact information in your profile, so it's a good idea to include one or two ways people can contact you and your website right at the top of your description.

The profile page also asks questions about where you live, your work and your interests. The answers you put will be used to connect you with more topics of interest, so if you aren't interested in following questions related to your hometown, leave location blank. Experience is one section want to spend some time on. This is where you can put in absolutely anything of interest to you, and Quora will suggest related topics for you to follow.

You are on Quora to promote yourself and your work, so take the time to seek out every possible related topic. Get involved in broad topics and detailed subtopics. Don't get too focused though. You never know where you will make a contact, and people like having a personal connection. Pick at least a few topics that aren't business related, but are things you are interested or passionate about. You never know when the folks following you because they like what you have to say about sports or fashion will need a professional contact in your field.

When you are satisfied with your profile and have chosen all the topics you want to follow for now, head back to your homepage. At the bottom of the right hand column, click on the links to connect your social media to Quora. Your answers and questions on Quora can then be shared on those social media sites. You can choose to have them shared automatically or you can only share specific activity. It's up to you.

ADJUSTING ACCOUNT SETTINGS

If you would like, you can go up to the top right corner of your home page and click on your name. Then choose "Account Settings" from the drop down menu. Here you can connect your blog to your Quora account, so your blog posts get posted to Quora. You can also adjust your email settings, so you only get emails from Quora when you want. Finally you can adjust your "Ask to Answer" settings. Ask to Answer is a way that people can ask experts in a topic to answer questions the expert might not be aware of. We'll be taking a closer look at Ask to Answer later.

Once you are satisfied with your settings, you are done setting up your account. Now it's time to get involved.

ASKING AND ANSWERING QUESTIONS

This is what Quora is about. The entire point of this site is sharing knowledge by asking and answering questions. For someone interested in promotion and making connections, answering questions is more of a focus than asking them, but asking questions can still sometimes be useful.

ASKING QUESTIONS

Asking questions can serve several purposes on Quora. It can help you connect with other professionals and experts in related fields, it can help you gather information for your work and projects, it can help you learn more about running and promoting your work, and it can give you insights into more advanced areas of your field. While the focus of this book is using Quora to promote yourself and your business, don't ignore the potential value of Quora as a tool to learn and expand your areas of knowledge. Quora has answers from some of the leading experts in the world in various fields, and simply reading a few of these great answers can dramatically increase your knowledge pool.

It's also important to remember that promoting yourself is not a zero-sum game. By asking questions and giving other experts a chance to show their knowledge, you are still making connections. If you ask intelligent and interesting questions, people will follow you to see what new questions you come up with and what answers you find. Every connection is a possible conversion. Every avenue has value.

When you write a question, you will be asked the question you want answered, what topics the question goes in, and any comments or details you wish to share about the question. Be aware: anyone can add topics or comments to a question. The more topics you add, the more widely your question will be seen, but keep the topics you add relevant to the question. Similarly, the more details you add in the comments the more relevant the answers you get will be, but don't go into wall of text detail unless it is really necessary.

Once you have asked your question, you will have a chance to promote it. Promoting your question guarantees it will be seen by a certain number of people. In order to promote your question, you must spend Quora credits, which you get by answering questions, having your answers Upvoted and through a few other avenues. The number of credits you spend determines the number of people who will see your question. Promoted questions appear as the first activity in the Top Stories feed of people who are following the topic. Once the number of people you chose to promote the topic have also seen it, it will no longer appear there.

You can also ask other people to answer your question. Ask to Answer is Quora's way to encourage experts in a topic to answer new questions. When you create your question, you will be shown a list of people who have written answers in your topic. By spending Quora credits you can ask these people to answer your question—they receive the credits you spend as bonus credits if they answer.

You can also share your question on social media to get a wider audience.

ANSWERING QUESTIONS

There are several ways you can find questions to answer. You can type in the topic of the kinds of questions you'd like to answer in the search box, you can click on "Unanswered Questions" at the top of the right column, you can find an interesting question in your feed and click on in it to add your own answer, or at the very top of the page you can click on "Write" and then choose "Answer Questions" from the drop down menu. Each other these options will bring you to different questions you can choose to answer.

Don't be afraid to explore a bit. Answering unanswered questions can be a good way to get noticed, because your answer will be right at the top when anyone checks the question. On the other hand, if you answer a question that already has several answers, people who have already answered a question get notified when you add a new answer, and may come check out what you have to say.

When you answer a question, be as thorough as you can. Read over other answers that have already been given. If someone has already said what you would say, Upvote their answer and add a supporting comment. Make sure to use proper spelling and grammar and avoid industry related-jargon (unless it is clear from the question that the asker understands the jargon).

You can include links in your answers and comments. If you have something on your blog or website that is relevant to the question, definitely link to it! (If you don't already have some good content on a blog or website, now is the time to start adding it). Don't put links in that aren't relevant, and don't just link to your site. Remember, Quora is not going to get you direct conversion. Your purpose in answering has to be first to help people, and only second to promote yourself.

You will find a broad range of detail in answers; from 10,000 word incredibly detailed responses with pictures and videos embedded to a vague sentence or two. Steer between these two extremes. If you have to err, err on the side of providing *too much detail* rather than too little. Remember, the idea here is to brand yourself as the expert in your field. Experts provide detailed, helpful answers. Amateurs provide short, vague answers.

If your full answer to a question would turn into a book-length response, you can insert links, videos, and images to explain yourself as well. For example, if you were giving instructions on how to change an oil filter, I would recommend inserting images of each step along the way to help readers follow along. You could also simply insert a video of yourself changing an oil filter and explaining the process as you do it.

Always as you write, ask yourself *"Is my answer responding to the question?"* and *"Is my answer providing new and helpful information for the asker?"* If you can't say "Yes" to both those questions, move on. **Remember, your goal is to provide value and help people. If you can't do that by answering a question, you're better off not answering at all.**

Once your answer is posted, people can comment on it and edit it. You will receive notifications of both of these things.

When someone comments on your answer, they may be asking for clarification, they may be disagreeing with you, or they may be supporting you. In general, it is a good idea to respond to comments. Be polite and clear in your responses. Comments are a great way to have a conversation with people, so don't be afraid to engage the folks who comment, just do so in a professional manner.

Much of the time, when someone suggests an edit on an answer, it will be grammar related: someone who found a few out of place apostrophes. No one can edit your answer directly, all they can do is suggest edits to you. You will get a notice, and a chance to compare your original answer with the suggested edits. If you want to approve the edits, your answer will be updated. If you don't want to approve the edits, your answer will stay unchanged.

You can also edit your answer yourself at any time. If you learn more information that would be relevant, if a link you included gets broken, or if there is one point where you realize a lot of people need clarification, you can change your answer as needed. If you change your answer too much, then it won't fit with the comments and may confuse the people who read it later, so try to keep new changes from altering the basic ideas of the answer—but if you need to totally re-write your answer for accuracy or clarity do it.

Asking and answering questions are your primary means of connecting with people on Quora. People who like your questions or answers will follow you, click on links you include, and look for other things you have to say. By replying to comments you can start a conversation and develop relationships, and that is the most powerful part of the site.

CHAPTER 3
COMBINING QUORA AND OTHER SOCIAL MEDIA CHANNELS

ᘓᘒᘔ

C ombining social media is always a great way to improve the reach and effectiveness of your activity. However Quora has some weaknesses when it comes to meshing with other social media. To get the most benefit from combining Quora and social media, you need to put some thought and preparation into how, when and more importantly where you share.

CONNECTING WITH OTHER SOCIAL MEDIA

As you saw in the section on setting up your account, Quora makes it easy to connect your Quora account to some social media outlets. Specifically, they have built in options for connecting Facebook, Twitter and

LinkedIN accounts with Quora. At the time of this writing they do not have a means to directly connect Quora to your G+ feed. You can connect Quora to a Google account if you do so when you create the Google account. If you don't create your Quora account through your Google account, there is no way to connect it later.

Presumably, Quora will be adding other social media connections as time goes on. Certainly the growth of G+ makes it an important social media to establish connections with. For now, if you want to share Quora activity on media other than Facebook, Twitter and LinkedIN you will need to do so manually.

As mentioned before, you can set Quora to automatically share your activity with your connected social media or to only share when you specifically want to. In general, it is better to not use automatic sharing. First, because you don't want to spam your followers on other media with everything you do on Quora. Second, because sometimes there may be answers that you don't want to share—maybe you decide to answer a question on a personal topic that you don't want shared on you LinkedIN account or perhaps you have decided to comment on something anonymously. Having that anonymous comment posted on Facebook under your name would rather defeat the purpose of being anonymous! Finally, social media is most effective if you are selective in your sharing. Having the same links come up on your

Facebook, Twitter and LinkedIN all the time can annoy your followers, instead you want to target what you share to s specific audience.

Quora's Big Social Media Weakness

The major weakness of combining Quora with social media is the fact that people can't see anything on Quora without creating an account. This is especially a problem for short form social media such as Twitter. No matter how intriguing the headline is, few people will appreciate clicking on a link to find they can't see what is on the other side until they create an account on a website they know nothing about. Which is why this is just about the last time you will see Twitter mentioned in this guide.

Facebook and LinkedIN, which allow longer posts and can share the entirety of the answer or question you are linking to, are more useful. When you share an answer you write on LinkedIN or Facebook, people can read the question and the full answer you have created in your feed on your social media profile. They cannot read other answers or comments to your answers. However, comments on social media can create a new conversation about your answer, and people can choose to share or link to your answer themselves, if they find it interesting or useful.

BENEFITS OF COMBINING QUORA AND OTHER SOCIAL MEDIA

Combining Quora with social media can build your networks in both locations. Someone who likes a Quora answer you share to Facebook may join and follow you on Quora to see what else you have to say. Alternatively, someone who likes the answer you share to Facebook may share it with their social media networks, bringing your name and ideas to the attention of new people, who may then choose to send you a friend request, expanding your Facebook network.

Other useful social media sites that can be effectively combined with Quora include Reddit, Digg and StumbleUpon.

EFFECTIVE SHARING ON SOCIAL MEDIA

When choosing what to share where, make sure to ask yourself three questions: "Is this activity relevant to this network?" (What is relevant to your business associates on LinkedIN will be different from what is relevant to friends or fans on Facebook.) "Will this activity grab the attention of people on this network?" Finally, "how much have I shared with this network today?"

By answering these questions, you can avoid accidentally spamming your social media networks with uninteresting, irrelevant information, or just oversharing.

Social media and Quora are both tools. Used together they can be very effective. Just go in with your eyes open and always, always, always make sure what you are sharing will benefit your network.

Interacting with Other Users

If you are using Quora to promote yourself or your business, then interacting with other users is a critical part of your Quora experience. These interactions can be brief or ongoing. The most important thing is to make them repeat. The more often someone sees your name, the more likely they are to remember you. The more often they see you have something interesting or relevant to say, the more likely they are to seek you out when they need information or assistance.

There are several ways of interacting with people on Quora. In general, they can be divided into proactive interactions and reactive interactions. Proactive interactions include commenting on someone else's answer. Reactive interactions include responding when someone else comments on an answer of yours.

Proactive Interactions

Proactive interactions are a powerful way to get attention. By seeking out other users and initiating contact, you are creating the interaction and telling them that they have something to say that you find interesting or valuable. Everyone likes to hear that.

There are several ways to interact proactively with other Quora members. The easiest way to do this is to comment on the answers that other people leave. Other options are: following someone, sending a message, and asking someone to answer a question.

When you comment on someone else's answer, you are starting a discussion with that person. The discussion may take any number of turns depending on how you and the other person approach it. If you disagree with someone, and express that disagreement in a constructive way, you can start a good dialogue, and the other person might find your viewpoint interesting enough to seek you out and follow your activity. On the other hand, a comment that expresses agreement without providing anything of substance is likely to be skimmed. At best you might get a quick reply, "Thank you for your support." And that is the end of the interaction.

Now, the point is not that it is better to disagree than to agree. The point is that constructive comments are more likely to lead to valuable interaction. When you leave a comment, try to make it something that creates an opening for further discussion, or that adds further information to the answer already given.

Following someone is a passive form of proactive interaction. Sometimes the people you follow will follow you back, but don't follow someone expecting that. Instead, look at following someone as a gateway to more opportunities to interact with them.

When you follow someone, their activities become part of your feed. So anytime they ask a question, answer a question, put up a blog post or vote on someone else's activity, you will see it. And each time they appear in your feed, it provides an opportunity to interact with them. You can answer their questions, comment on their answers and read their blog posts.

Sending a message is one of the underutilized methods of interaction on Quora. It is hard to predict how someone will react to an unsolicited message. That said, if you and another Quora user have been interacting frequently, commenting on each other's answers, asking and answering questions, etc., then it would definitely be appropriate to send them a message if you find something that you think they might be interested in or have a question you want to ask privately.

Asking to Answer appears to be a program that is unique to Quora. As noted earlier, when you interact on Quora you earn Quora credits. By spending these credits, you can ask specific people to answer a question you are interested in. When you write a question, or visit an unanswered question, Quora will give you a brief list of people who have demonstrated knowledge in the topic that you can Ask to Answer (along with how many credits it will cost to ask them) and will give the option of searching for someone else to ask. If you know that someone is knowledgeable on a topic, sending them an Ask to Answer request can be way to let them know that you recognize and value their expertise.

Promoting a question or answer is our last means of proactive interaction. If you choose to, you can spend some of those Quora credits to make sure that your question or answer is seen by a large number of people. The number of credits you spend determines how many people see the promoted activity. Promoted activity will only show up in the feeds of people who have followed the topic, but it will show up at the top of their feeds. Promoting a question you ask can be a good way to get as wide a variety of answers as possible.

I recommend promoting an answer you have given that you think has great value to a wide variety of people. This can be a great way to get that answer (and your name) in front of people who might never have seen it otherwise. Some of those people may choose to follow you or comment on the answer—or follow a relevant link back to your website! Promoting your own high value answers on Quora is probably the best way to use your Credits for marketing.

REACTIVE INTERACTIONS

Reactive interactions are the times when someone else initiates something and you respond. If someone asks a question and you answer, you are reacting. Same if someone comments on your answer and you reply. Reactive interaction leaves the initiative in the other person's hands—but is also tells them that you were listening to what they said and thought it was worth responding too.

Answering a question is the most common form of reactive interaction—after all, if people didn't answer questions, there wouldn't be a Quora! By frequently answering questions in topics you are knowledgeable about, you can become a recognized voice on that topic. This can lead people to seek you out, send you Ask to Answer requests, or follow you. If they come across you in other areas of the web, they will be more likely to follow you or send a friend request, because they already know you have something to say that they want to hear.

Replying to comments is not as powerful as answering questions, but it is more personal. You are having direct interaction with the person who commented. This makes it more likely that person will remember you, interact with you in the future and choose to follow you on Quora. By replying to comments that they leave for you, you are saying that the time and effort they took is appreciated and their thoughts were worth responding too.

Following back is another form of reactive interaction. Someone chose to follow you, and you responded by following them. Over time, you will probably interact with this person frequently as both of you respond to the activity of the other that comes up in your feeds.

Finally, you can respond to Ask to Answer requests. Simply answering the question is a very indirect form of interaction—the person who asked you may have simply chosen your name from the list Quora provides and may not know anything about you. However, you can make this a more personal interaction by sending them a message, "Thanks for asking me to answer X question. It's an interesting topic that I enjoy writing about."

Making effective use of Quora requires being both proactive and reactive in your interactions. It means seeking out people to build connections with, and responding to the people who seek you out. Interacting is how people learn to recognize your name and expertise. So for successful promotion, make sure that interacting with people is a large part of your Quora experience.

YOUR QUORA BLOG

Blogging is a powerful social media tool, and Quora recognizes that. If you don't already have a blog, don't worry. Quora provides you with one.

Unlike a regular blog, your Quora blog is only accessible to other Quora users. However, that doesn't make it any less valuable within the Quora community. And if you have linked your Quora account to other social media, you can share your Quora blog with those networks as well.

The Quora blog is the "next step" in building your Quora network and reputation. While your answers and questions will show up in the feed of anyone who is following the topic, your blog posts show up in the feed of the people who have chosen to follow you.

Your goal here is to make the blog valuable to these followers. To write about things that interest them, to share links to relevant websites and Quora questions and generally to provide value to them. When you provide value to your readers, they come back for more.

Everyone on Quora automatically has a blog they can post to. The URL for this blog is:

www.quora.com/user-name/Posts

The title of the blog will start out as "User Name's Posts" but the title can be edited at any time. You can add other people as authors to your blog, write a description of your blog, and set topics that the blog will be about.

You can also create additional Quora blog's by going to the "Write" tab at the very top of the screen and selecting "Create Blog" from the drop down menu. You'll be taken to a form where you enter the blog name, a custom URL, the topics your blog will cover and a brief description of your blog. Some of these can be edited later, but the URL can't.

Once your blog is created, you can add blog posts by going to the "Write" tab again and selecting "Write Post" from the drop down menu.

Creating a second Quora blog can be valuable if you have multiple business, want to write about widely divergent topics, or just enjoy keeping your personal and professional personas separate.

Your Quora blog settings allow you to change the blog from Public to Private to Secret. Secret blogs can only be viewed by blog members. Public blogs can be viewed by anyone. Private blogs will show up in other member's feeds, but the full posts can only be seen by people the blog owner approves. Which is the best option will vary from person to person, but in general if your goal is promoting yourself, keeping your blog public is usually a good idea.

Your blog should be updated regularly. It doesn't matter what schedule you update on, just try to find a schedule you can stick to. The more content you put up, the more chances you have for someone to find your blog, and you.

By working with other Quora users, you can create joint blogs. Inviting other people in your field to create a blog with you will enable you to have a blog that is constantly updated with new content, without putting too much of your time into maintaining the blog.

CHAPTER 4
QUORA BOUNTY OFFICE
AND OTHER
USER GENERATED PROGRAMS

ଊଔଈ

Quora likes to give its users relatively free rein to develop and grow the site. By trusting members to create and develop content for the site, Quora benefits from its members' creativity and drive to develop the community of which they want to be a part. Quora members who work together have created a number of programs to benefit and enhance the community.

One example of these programs that has particular uses for people who are promoting themselves and their work is the Quora Bounty Office.

THE QUORA BOUNTY OFFICE

The Quora Bounty Office is a relatively new part of Quora, but a potentially very useful one. The Quora Bounty Office exists so users can set rewards for other members who are able to meet certain criteria in answering hard-to-answer questions. Bounties are not common, but have high payouts, with some giving rewards as high as 4000 Quora credits.

For someone doing promotional work on Quora, there are two main uses for the bounty office. The first is as a means of gathering credits to promote questions and answers throughout the site. Remember that getting people to see your answers is one of the best ways to become known on Quora. Promoting a question or answer guarantees that it will be seen by a wide variety of people who might never be aware of it otherwise. Four thousand Quora credits can buy a lot of promotion.

The second use of the Quora Bounty Office is as an information gathering tool. There are lots of questions in running a business and building a marketing plan. Questions related to demographics, trends, new developments, understanding withholding tax and much more. By posting a question to the Quora Bounty Office, with terms for the amount of detail and references you are looking for, you can "outsource" your question to people who are experts in the topic, while you focus on the work that you know best.

WHAT MAKES A BOUNTY?

Quora bounties have terms and conditions that must be met in order to earn the reward. Someone who wishes to place a bounty goes to the Quora Bounty Office and posts a bounty offer. The bounty offer needs to include the name of the person offering the bounty (the sponsor), the amount of credits offered, the question the bounty is for and any terms an answerer has to meet to receive the bounty. Common terms include "Must include references" or "First answer to receive 5 upvotes." Finally, the bounty posting has to include a brief argument of why the question is worthy of a bounty.

Bounties have been posted for a wide variety of questions. But relatively few total bounties have been distributed.

PROGRAMS SIMILAR TO QBO

The Quora Bounty Office was created by several Quora users who wanted to a system to get unique and challenging questions answered. Similar programs include the Quora Credit Co-Op and Quora Topic Incubator.

User generated programs like these are scattered throughout Quora, but are unfortunately hard to find. Some, like QBO and Topic Incubator are based in Quora blogs. Others, like the Credit Co-Op are built by creating a new Quora topic (in this case the Quora

Credit Co-Op topic) where questions are asked with the goal of organizing the project and getting it off the ground.

CREATING YOUR OWN USER GENERATED PROJECT

If approached properly, projects like these can be helpful in promoting yourself and even more helpful in gathering information for your business. However, because they are so scattered and difficult to find, they are a very hit-or-miss option. Not enough people know about them and use them for them to become truly self-sustaining.

For the dedicated Quora user who wants to self-promote on Quora, these projects offer a template for a unique way to interact. By gathering together others with similar interests, you can create your own user-generated program on Quora. One of the weaknesses of the above mentioned programs is that its extreme broadness creates a real challenge in marketing them on Quora's topic-driven promotion system. However, it would be very easy for four or five web developers to get together and create a user generated program dedicated to answering questions about web design. They might offer a reward to people who can ask questions that stump them, commit to making sure that there were no unanswered questions in the Web Design topic, build a Quora blog as a web design FAQ with links to their answers on popular questions in the Web Design topic or much more. Because the project would be topic-specific, it would be easily found by people searching for activity related to web design and could be promoted throughout the web design topic.

Those same web designers might also network outside of Quora, sending people with questions to their Quora FAQ, referring business to each other or even gathering their Quora blog posts into an eBook about web design they could offer as a free download to their clients.

How useful projects like this might be will vary widely. They take more time and commitment than standard Quora interactions, because you need to find others to build the project with you, create an agreement for what the project will do and how you will do it, divide responsibilities, and keep up with the actual work of the project.

However these projects also offer opportunities to network with other professionals in your field, increased visibility on Quora, and other unique opportunities to promote your Quora activity on other social media.

Try to have a plan before jumping into a project like this. Be prepared to promote it all over to gather the interest to make it self sustaining (another use for those bounties!) and be sure that you and your partners are able to put in the necessary time and effort. But if you can pull together a user generated project, you will have a powerful tool for promoting yourself and making new connections throughout Quora.

LEVERAGING QUORA TO PROMOTE YOUR WORK

Throughout this book we've looked at a variety of different ways you can use Quora to promote yourself and your business. Now we are going to pull it all together. The important thing to remember is that ultimately Quora is a networking tool—it is not going to get you any immediate returns, but over time it can help you bring in new contacts and new customers.

The basic rule of online promotion is conversion. You want to convert social media followers into website views, website views into direct contacts and direct contacts into sales or clients. From Quora, then, your goal is to bring people to your website. With a strong website, those visitors can in time be converted to customers or clients.

The first step of conversion on Quora is grabbing people's attention. This is where answering questions and commenting on other people's answers is crucial. In some of these answers and comments, you can include a link to your website. More often, your goal is to get people who read your answers or comments to choose to follow you. The key for this stage is to be interesting and active. The more often people see your name and think, "Hey, this person has some neat things to say!" the more likely they are to follow you.

Getting followers is the first step in converting fellow Quora users to customers. Because of the importance of answering questions and being active on the site, focusing your answers in topics related to your business can be powerful. You want Quora to be promoting you as someone to Ask to Answer. You want to have lots of Upvotes on your answers to bring you up on the Top Stories feed. You want to develop a reputation as someone who knows what they are talking about. Don't forget to promote your best answers and interact with people in other ways!

Once you have followers, you want to bring them to your website. You have several ways to do this: through links in your answers and comments, through your profile page, and through your blog.

Build up the content on your website so it is relevant and interesting for readers. Develop articles or an FAQ list you can link to when people ask something related to your field. Make your website an information gold mine. This gives you lots of legitimate options for putting links in your answers and comments. Remember: only include a link if it is relevant to the question and will provide value to the reader. "For more information, go here" links are good. "By the way, check out my website" links are not.

Your profile is the place to put "By the way, check out my website!" Include a link to your website in your description, with a bit of information about what is on the website and why people should check it out. If people start to follow you because they like your answers, and your profile says they can find more of the same on your website, they are more likely to check your website out.

Your blog is your power hitter. It is the one part of Quora that you can really personalize and make about you and about promoting yourself. Your followers will see blog posts in your feed. If your blog posts are interesting, they will read them and start looking for them. End every blog post with a call to action, "If you want to learn more about DIY plumbing, visit my website." "If you have termites don't wait to call the exterminators until it's too late. Check here for people in your area." "Website design is a constantly changing field, if you are interested in a quote on a redesign for your website, click here."

Don't make every call to action lead to your website—some can lead to informational websites, online petitions or other relevant sites. But if people get in the habit of answering your calls to action, they are more likely to respond when you call to action leads them to your website.

COMBINING SOCIAL MEDIA AND QUORA FOR BUSINESS PROMOTION

We talked earlier about how Quora and social media can combine to support each other and build your various networks. Now let's look specifically at using that combination to leverage business.

If you are largely in a business-to-business field, then LinkedIN is one of the more powerful social media sites available to you. By sharing answers and blog posts from Quora on your LinkedIN activity, you can demonstrate your knowledge and experience to people who are interested in learning more about you and your business. This can build your reputation on LinkedIN and increase your chance of getting new connections and new business opportunities. Make sure the answers and blog posts you share are those that provide value to your LinkedIN network. You want your connections to see you are a source of possible solutions. By promoting the ways you have provided solutions to others (your Quora answers) and sharing your knowledge (your blog posts) in relevant topics you can show your LinkedIN connections how your services can benefit them.

Facebook is your go-to site for direct-to-consumer business. Your goals here are the same as on LinkedIN—use Quora answers and blog posts to showcase your knowledge and how you can provide solutions for the people reading your Facebook feed. That said, Facebook is largely an entertainment site. Where with LinkedIN your focus should be on providing valuable information and demonstrating experience, on Facebook you want to be entertaining. Answers which include amusing anecdotes from your work, stories of your education and the occasional "How to do this interesting thing" post, will go over well and get shared widely. Long rambling posts, not so much. On Facebook, you don't want to be promoting yourself too directly. Instead, you want to people to remember you. "I need to talk to someone about building a website. Hey, didn't Janet share that story from a web designer on Facebook yesterday? He sounded like someone I could work with."

Whatever your social media of choice, remember your goal is to bring readers to you. Make sure that your posts and profile contain either easily recognizable contact information or obvious links to your website.

Always remember to be professional and polite. This doesn't mean you need to be formal—a relaxed and approachable person often has an easier time making connections. Don't be afraid to be friendly or to share personal stories and experiences. Just remember when you share them that you want what you share to reflect well on you and your business. Sometimes that means being able to laugh at yourself and your business' growing pains. Other times, that means being able to stay polite and courteous while dealing with a troll.

CHAPTER 5
INTERESTING AND USEFUL FEATURES OF QUORA YOU PROBABLY DON'T KNOW ABOUT

৩৪৩

Even though most Quora users don't know it, Quora has a LOT of functionality on the site – probably just as much as Facebook. Many of these features are incredibly helpful – if you know about them. Some will save you time, some will help you find information faster, and others are just really cool or interesting.

SEARCH PAGE

You can search for any questions, answers or topics:

www.quora.com/search?q=quora

MONITOR QUESTIONS

Monitoring questions is a great way to stay in the loop if you want to learn more about a specific topic. It's also a great way to spy on the competition and see how they're answering questions.

**www.quora.com/
Monitoring-Questions-on-Quora**

MANAGE TOPICS

By managing a topic, you can add aliases, merge two topics that are the same, delete topics, and more.

www.quora.com/Business/manage

ANSWER CHANGE LOG

Quora keeps a log of all changes to answers. Some users don't like it, but it provides a lot of transparency and openness to the system. It can also help keep users from stealing other people's ideas, or crowdsourcing responses, to make their answer appear the best or most comprehensive.

USER ENDORSEMENTS PAGE

You can endorse other users on Quora, and they can endorse you. This rarely used feature can be a great way to get more exposure and add credibility to your Quora profile.

See:

www.quora.com/
Tom-Corson-Knowles/endorsements

REDIRECTING QUESTIONS AND ANSWERS

You can redirect questions and/or answers on Quora. This is useful if there are two questions that are basically the same. Generally, you should redirect the question with the least answers to the question with the most answers.

You can also redirect answers if you feel that answer is applicable to a different question.

MARK AS BEST ANSWER

You can mark an answer as Best Answer and that will feature that answer at the top, as well as let people know it's the best answer.

EDITING QUESTIONS, AND QUESTION DETAILS

You can edit your questions and question details at any time. If you're not getting any good answers, try changing the question or adding in question details that might help potential answering members!

ANSWER SUMMARIES

If you get a lot of great answers to your question, you can add the main highlights in an Answer Summary, which will then appear just under the question and above the answers. This can help other users get the information a lot faster rather than reading through all the answers.

NOT FOR REPRODUCTION

Quora has a settings button under each of your answers. If you click it, there's an option to mark your answer as "Not for Reproduction." If you mark it not for reproduction, you will have to give a reason why you don't want the answer reproduced. Then, the words "Not for Reproduction" will appear next to your answer. Your reason for making it Not for Reproduction will be shown in your answer log as well.

BROWSING BEST ANSWERS

Click on any topic and on the topic page you'll find a "best answers" section. This section usually contains truly inspired stuff. If you ever find yourself with some free time, you should go to topics that interest you on Quora and read the best questions.

CHAPTER 6
ADVANCED QUORA MARKETING STRATEGIES

cs૪ல

As a content creator, marketer or expert in your field, one of the easiest things to do is simply share your knowledge and expertise. But sitting in your office staring at a computer screen isn't often the best way to inspire your creativity and generate amazing content that will have customers lining up to buy from you.

That's where Quora really shines. Because every time you login to Quora and browse through the questions in your area of expertise, you'll see the *exact problems your potential customers are having*. And, since you already know how to solve these problems, all you have to do is write the answer to the question!

If you're a blogger, writer, author, public relations expert or marketer, Quora will make it *easy* for you to get your message out there and to find the exact message your market wants and needs.

Let me show you how...

USING QUORA FOR MARKET RESEARCH

What if there was one website you could go to where you could find *every important question your target customer has ever asked?* Luckily for us, that site now exists. It's Quora.

Let's say you're looking for new product or service ideas, but you're not quite sure exactly what people want or need that no other company is offering them. Quora can help you find this information.

STEP 1. DO A QUORA SEARCH FOR YOUR MARKET OR TOPIC

Let's say you're in the fashion business and you want to find new product or marketing ideas to grow your business. Simply type in "fashion" in the Quora search box.

Doing so led me to the "Fashion and Style" topic with over 500,000 followers at:

www.quora.com/Fashion-and-Style-1

You might also want to browse through other related topics even if they're smaller. Often, it's the smaller niche topics that can provide some of the best market research and new insights.

STEP 2. BROWSE THE BEST QUESTIONS AND ANSWERS

Next, it's time to do your market research. Here's what you should look for and why...

A) QUESTIONS WITH NO REAL ANSWERS

Questions with no answers can be a great source for inspiration and new ideas because it means a potential customer has a problem *and no one else knows how to solve it.* If you solve that problem, assuming it's a big enough problem, that customer and many more will be forced to buy from you because you'll be the only one in the world offering a solution to that problem!

B) QUESTIONS WITH DOZENS OR HUNDREDS OF ANSWERS

Questions that get a lot of answers and views mean it's a hot topic. Chances are, that out of a hundred answers, you might find one or two that provide a truly unique twist on current best practices or common sense. If you can take one of these new ideas and apply them to your product or service, you just might be able to come up with something unique and totally different than what anyone else is offering in your market.

c) Ask your own questions

If you can't find what you're looking for, go ahead and ask your own questions for market research. Here are some examples of great market research questions:

> *What's your biggest challenge with [insert your topic, market or product]?*
>
> *What new product or service would you invent for [insert your topic, market or product] if you could?*
>
> *What do you hate about [insert your topic, market or product]?*
>
> *What do you love about [insert your topic, market or product]?*
>
> *What problems are there with [insert your topic, market or product] that most people don't know about or understand?*

These are just a few quick suggestions. Brainstorm with your team on more great market research questions you can ask on Quora. You'll never know what one answer could change your business and your life forever until you ask!

USING QUORA FOR REPUTATION MANAGEMENT AND PROACTIVE CUSTOMER SERVICE

Many big companies and brands still don't realize that their products and services are being discussed on

Quora. That's a huge mistake and a lost opportunity for them. But it can be a gold mine for you!

The first thing you'll want to do is type in your name, your company's name and any product or service brand names you own in Quora to see if anything comes up. If there are already questions about you or your company, go ahead and answer them intelligently.

For example, there's a question on Quora, "Is Coca-Cola toxic?" Maybe Coca-Cola doesn't feel like it needs to address such issues, but if you're a small business, you can't afford not to answer a question like that! Provide your customers with the best, most up-to-date information you can, and they will appreciate the information and your proactivity in responding to their concerns.

You can also have a friend ask your own questions for you, or just ask them anonymously yourself about your products or services. Then answer the question as thoroughly as you can. This is being proactive about customer service. If someone does have a problem in the future and types that question into Quora, it'll pop up and they'll see your answer right away.

If you have an FAQ on your website, you ought to ask and answer all of these questions on Quora yourself. If it's important enough to have that information on your website, it should be on Quora too. That's being proactive about customer service.

TURNING QUESTIONS INTO BLOG POSTS

Many questions on Quora will be so basic and fundamental to understanding a particular topic or subject that you'll want to devote some serious effort into writing the answer. Instead of a few sentences, your answer might contain several paragraphs and look like a long blog post. That's perfect!

And here's how to use these foundational questions to build your web traffic *and* your exposure on Quora at the same time.

STEP 1. FIND A "FOUNDATIONAL" QUESTION

Remember, foundational questions are those that are so crucial to understand for your potential customer that it deserves being answered thoroughly.

STEP 2. WRITE THE BEST ANSWER POSSIBLE

Next, you're going to write the best answer you possibly can. You might want to bring in helpful pictures and video tutorials, bullet points, well-designed formatting, and more to make your answer the best it can possibly be.

STEP 3. PUBLISH THE ANSWER ON YOUR BLOG FIRST!

Next, you're going to publish the answer on your own blog or website *first!* Here's why...

We're talking about truly *great* answers here. These answers are so good that, if it was a blog post, it would probably go viral and bring a ton of traffic to your website. And, since the blog post would be answering one of the most important questions your target customers could ever ask, this traffic will be highly targeted and convert into buyers. That's why you want this content on your blog.

And you want to post it on your blog *before* you post it on Quora so that Google and other search engines will index it on your site first and foremost. If you post the answer on Quora first and then on your blog later, search engines will see duplicate content on your site, which won't help you when it comes to attracting search traffic. But, if you post on your site first and let Google index your page before posting on Quora, you'll get all the search engine benefits of the article as well as the extra traffic to your site *and* the extra exposure on Quora.

Note: You will probably want to edit the post on your blog slightly so that it sounds like a real blog post and not an answer to a single person on Quora.

Step 4. Post the Answer on Quora

Once you've posted the article on your blog and shared it on social media, you should wait 3-4 hours at least before posting the answer on Quora. If your site gets lots of search engine traffic, 3-4 hours will be plenty of time for Google to index your new post. On the other hand, if your blog is brand new and gets little to no search traffic, you may want to wait 24-48 hours before posting the answer on Quora to make sure Google has had enough time to index your new blog post.

CHAPTER 7
LIMITATIONS OF QUORA

 C3§80

As much as I love Quora, I must admit there are several limitations to the platform right now, and I think it's only fair to you to let you know about them.

Quora is unmistakably a useful site for establishing and online reputation and making connections that can lead to business opportunities. However, it isn't perfect. Below are the major limitations I've found with using Quora to promote my business.

VIEW RESTRICTIONS

We mentioned this one earlier and it is probably one of the most annoying limitations of Quora. The inability of anyone without a Quora account to see anything on

Quora makes it difficult to use Quora as a tool outside of the existing Quora community.

The existing community is large, and is constantly growing. And the ability to share Quora activity on other social media counters this limitation to an extent.

On the other hand, this restriction means you can't link your website directly to your Quora blog, or use Twitter effectively in combination with Quora (because all your Twitter followers would have to be logged in to Quora in order to see the content).

If your target demographic is widely represented on Quora, this restriction won't have a large impact on you. If they aren't, it may. Unfortunately, there is no easy way to identify which demographics are widely represented in the Quora community right now. I suspect Quora will be releasing more information on user demographics as it grows.

I'm only speculating here, but based on my experience with the site, I would say that the average Quora user has more years of college education and advanced degrees than the average American, and their incomes are above the median. If you sell luxury goods or products, business-to-business services or target a highly educated or high earning clientele, Quora will be a great place to reach your target market and grow your business.

GEOGRAPHY

Unless you run a tourist-related business, it is very difficult to build connections on Quora if your work is geographically restricted. Quora does have topics related to specific locations, but most questions in those topics are related to sights of interest, politics or where to find good restaurants. An accountant from Charleston could get involved in topics related to accounting and in topics related to Charleston, but it would be difficult for them to connect with people from Charleston who are interested in finding an accountant.

Sharing work-related Quora activity on other social media can still help you build a reputation on those networks. For instance, that same accountant who shares their Quora activity on LinkedIN may impress people who visit their profile with their knowledge and experience, and increase their chances of getting hired. However this is a major limitation of Quora, making it a far better platform for internet based businesses that can work with clients from anywhere.

Lack of Contact Information

Most social media sites include in your profile at least a few ways for people to contact you. LinkedIN profiles can have list after list of emails, websites, social media contacts, phone numbers... Quora doesn't really seem interested in enabling people to connect outside of Quora. The link to send someone a message within

Quora is hidden away in a corner—and there is no place to put your contact information on the profile.

You can counter this by putting your contact information front and center in your personal description. Don't put a long list, just the one or two ways you most prefer people to contact you, and your website.

It's Compulsive and Distracting

In many ways, this is a problem familiar from any social media site. It is just way to easy to get lost on Quora, jumping from question to question, reading answers, commenting on other peoples writings and learning a lot of interesting stuff. In a way this is a good thing, after all the more you are involved the more connections you make, right?

But don't get lost. Try to keep your activity as on topic as possible, and don't spend more than a half an hour or so on Quora each day. If you have a regular social media schedule, integrate Quora into it. If not, create a specific schedule for working on Quora. Do not let Quora, or any social media, distract you from doing your actual work. After all, marketing is important, it brings in new customers—but remember the old saying: make new friends, but keep the old; one is silver and the other gold. Your established customers and your work for them takes priority over the use of social media every day of the week.

IS QUORA RIGHT FOR YOU?

There are a lot of ways to promote yourself on the internet, and only so much time available. There just isn't time in the week to spend on all the possible social media outlets, never mind blogging, forums and plain old advertising.

So how can you know if Quora is the right site for you to invest your time in? Especially when whatever options you choose, it will be months before you start seeing returns on your investment?

Before you even consider what is right for your promotional efforts, think of what is write for *you*. Are you comfortable using Quora? Does its setup and function make sense to you? Do you have an easy time answering questions and sharing information? If not, it doesn't matter how useful Quora might be to your business, this is not the right tool for you.

On the other hand, if trying to come up with pithy sayings for Twitter drives you crazy, and you aren't sure what to do with your Facebook feed, but enjoy helping people learn and sharing solutions for people's difficulties, then Quora may be perfect for you.

And if you are one of those social media mavens who slots right into every new social media tool like you were born there... well, what are you waiting for?

If you aren't sure if Quora is a good fit for you, go ahead and create an account. Use your personal email, don't link it to your work social media just yet. Explore, have fun and see how you like it.

Once you know that Quora is a good fit for you, it's time to take a hard look at your business. Are the topics on Quora that relate to your business very active? Or are there only new questions a couple times a month? Does the geographic reach of your business work with Quora's non-local focus, or do you need a site that lets your promote yourself specifically to people in your area?

Is your work something that is easy to discuss with clients and convey information in words? Let's face it, audio-visual professionals can talk with each other all day long about technique and the best programs to use. But the best way to connect with a potential client is to show them your work – which isn't possible on Quora.

Take a look at the questions being asked in your topics. Are they the kinds of questions you can connect with your business? Are they being asked by the people you want to connect with and promote yourself to? Or are they mostly being asked by other people in your field?

Quora can still be a valuable resource, even if it isn't a good tool for promoting your business. But it's best to go in knowing how you want to use it. This isn't a complete discussion of how to tell if Quora is the right place to promote your business – but it will get you started thinking in the right direction.

Whatever you decide, make sure you go in with a plan. Set goals, schedule activity, and plan concrete steps to get where you want to be. But don't forget to be flexible!

CHAPTER 8
MAKING QUORA
WORK FOR YOU

꧁꧂

That's it. Everything you need to know to get started on Quora, and using Quora to promote yourself and your business. Stay active, answer questions, and make connections.

Quora is relatively new platform, and is still growing and adapting. As you explore, keep your eyes open for changes that may create new opportunities or alter existing practices. Experiment to find the ratio of answers, comments, and blog posting that works for you. Play around with social media and how best to integrate your current social media plan with your Quora activity.

The possibilities may not be endless, but they are immense.

Aside from using Quora as a site to promote yourself and your business, don't overlook its value as an information resource. By watching the questions being asked in your field, you may be able to catch early trends and position yourself to take advantage of them. You can learn about other areas of your work outside your own specialties. You can connect with other people in your field and learn about their strategies and best practices. Explore, learn, answer, interact... and never stop questioning.

SPECIAL FACEBOOK GROUP

CȜ৪꙱

Come join our Facebook group just for readers like you who want to take their social media marketing to the next level. In this group we'll be sharing our successes, marketing tips and strategies with each other so that we can all continue to grow our businesses together.

This is also a fantastic group for finding joint venture partners and cross-promotion opportunities! Imagine the impact you could have collaborating with hundreds of other entrepreneurs from all over the world.

It's also a great place to get any marketing questions you have answered as well.

Come join us here on Facebook:

facebook.com/groups/EntrepreneurSuccessGroup

ABOUT THE AUTHOR

ⷩ

TOM CORSON-KNOWLES is the #1 Amazon best-selling author of *The Kindle Publishing Bible* and *How To Make Money With Twitter*, among others. He lives in Kapaa, Hawaii. Tom loves educating and inspiring other authors to succeed and live their dreams.

Learn more at: **Amazon.com/author/business**

Learn more about Tom's publishing company at:

www.TCKPublishing.com

CONNECT WITH TOM

Thank you so much for taking the time to read this book. I'm excited for you to start your path to creating the life of your dreams as a Kindle author.

If you have any questions of any kind, feel free to contact me directly at Tom@TCKPublishing.com

You can follow me on Twitter: @JuiceTom

And connect with me on Facebook: on.fb.me/W8fA7B

You can check out my publishing blog for the latest updates here: TCKpublishing.com

I'm wishing you the best of health, happiness, and success!

Here's to you!

Tom Corson-Knowles

OTHER BOOKS BY TOM CORSON-KNOWLES

಼಼

Systemize, Automate, Delegate

Ninja Book Marketing Strategies

The Kindle Publishing Bible

The Kindle Writing Bible

The Kindle Formatting Bible

How To Make Money With Twitter

The Blog Business Book

101 Ways To Start A Business For Less Than $1,000

Facebook For Business Owners

Rich by 22: How To Achieve Business Success at an Early Age

How To Reduce Your Debt Overnight

Index

A

B

C